Raintree is an imprint of Capstone Global Library Limited, a company incorporated
in England and Wales having its registered office at 7 Pilgrim Street, London,
EC4V 6LB — Registered company number: 6695582

www.raintree.co.uk
myorders@raintree.co.uk

Editorial Credits:
Editor: Shelly Lyons
Designer: Ted Williams
Art Director: Nathan Gassman
Production Specialist: Tori Abraham

ISBN 978-1-4062-8896-4 (paperback)
18 17 16 15 14
10 9 8 7 6 5 4 3 2 1

British Library Cataloguing in Publication Data
A full catalogue record for this book is available from the British Library.

Acknowledgements
We would like to thank the following for permission to reproduce photographs: Design
Elements: Shutterstock: ailin1, AllAnd, hugolacasse, Studiojumpee

The illustrations in this book were created traditionally, with digital colouring.

We would like to thank Elizabeth Tucker Gould, Professor of English, Binghamton
University for her invaluable help in the preparation of this book.

Printed and bound in China.

Scooby-Doo and the gang were returning from a
walk in the park. Suddenly, Scooby-Doo's ears perked up.

"What's wrong, Scoob?" asked Shaggy.

"Rerewolf!" barked Scooby. "Up there!"

"Really?" asked Velma.

"Are you sure?" asked Fred. "Do you know what a werewolf is?"

Before they change, they look like ordinary people. But after they change, they look like wolves!

RIKES!

"Maybe," said Daphne. "Stories say they live in houses and apartment buildings-just like humans. Werewolves are found all around the world."

"How do people become werewolves?" asked Shaggy.

"Legends tell us some people become werewolves through magic," said Velma.

"Others change when a werewolf bites them," added Fred. "Or when they drink water that a wolf has touched."

"When do werewolves change from humans into wolves?" asked Shaggy.

"Only at night," said Fred.

"When the moon is full," said Daphne. "Like tonight. Look for a werewolf in the moonlight, and listen for its howling."

"Like, do werewolves have superpowers?" asked Shaggy.

"You bet," answered Daphne. "Legends say they are really strong."

"And don't forget about their senses," said Velma. "They have extraordinary vision, hearing and sense of smell."

"Werewolves are vicious hunters," said Daphne.

"True," said Fred. "And once they taste blood, they crave it."

"Also, unless they die while in human form," said Velma, "werewolves are immortal."

"They rever die?" gasped Scooby. "Ruh, roh!"

"Rolfsrane?" asked Scooby.

"A plant with a beautiful purple flower," said Velma. "It's very poisonous. That's why people don't grow it in flowerbeds."

How can werewolves be stopped?
Long ago doctors gave them medicine or performed surgery.

Some people thought saying the werewolf's real name three times in a row would break the magic curse.

Today they say if you shoot a werewolf with a silver bullet, you stop the beast forever.

YOW!

"Rerewolf!" shouted Scooby.

Fred looked at Shaggy and laughed.

"Boy is this burrito hot!" cried Shaggy.

GLOSSARY

burrito Mexican food that is a tortilla rolled around a filling

curse evil spell meant to harm someone

immortal able to live forever

legend a story handed down from earlier times; it is often based in fact, but is not entirely true

transform change form

vicious fierce or dangerous

BOOKS

Monster Wars: Vampires vs. Werewolves, Michael John O'Hearn (Raintree 2012)

Mythical Creatures: Werewolves, Rebecca Rissman (Raintree 2011)

WEBSITES

myths.e2bn.org/mythsandlegends/
Browse this website to discover new myths and legends and use the myth map to see where in the world these stories have been collected from.

www.storymuseum.org.uk
Search the story museum for stories of werewolves and listen to audio retellings of well known myths and legends from around the world.

INDEX